Pieces from the Long Afternoon

by Monica Ochtrup

Minnesota Voices Project Number 46

NEW RIVERS PRESS 1991

Library of Congress Catalog Card Number 90-61095
ISBN 0-89823-125-6
Edited by C.W. Truesdale
Photographs by Bob Ochtrup
Frontispiece by Lynn Ball from the mixed-media installation: *Afternoon Rooms*, WARM Gallery, 1986
Book Design by Gaylord Schanilec
Typesetting by Peregrine Publications

Some of the poems in *Pieces From the Long Afternoon* have previously appeared in the following publications: Out of Hand Press and Judy Stone Nunneley (broadside), Pentagram and Out of Hand Press (broadside), *View From the Loft*, and the *Warm Journal*. Our thanks to the editors of these publications for allowing permission to reprint these poems here.

The author wishes to thank her editor, the poet C. W. Truesdale; Lynn Ball, Florence Dacey, Elizabeth Erickson, and Joyce Lyon for their attention to this work in manuscript; and Robert Battin for the correspondence in which many of these pieces began to find their way onto the page. Special thanks to the New York Botanical Garden for their permission to use the poster of the sunflower from Basilius Besler's *Hortus Eystettensis*.

The publication of *Pieces From the Long Afternoon* has been made possible by grant support from the Jerome Foundation, the Arts Development Fund of the United Arts Council, the Beverly J. and John A. Rollwagen Fund of the Minneapolis Foundation, Cray Research Foundation, the Elizabeth A. Hale Fund of the Minneapolis Foundation, the First Bank System Foundation, Liberty State Bank, the Star Tribune/Cowles Media Company, the Tennant Company Foundation, the Valspar Corporation, and the National Endowment for the Arts (with funds appropriated by the Congress of the United States). New Rivers Press also wishes to thank the Minnesota Non-Profts Assistance Fund for their invaluable support.

New Rivers Press books are distributed by

The Talman Company
150 – 5th Avenue
New York, NY 10011

Bookslinger
502 N. Prior Avenue
St. Paul, MN 55104

Pieces From the Long Afternoon has been manufactured in the United States of America for New Rivers Press (C.W. Truesdale, Editor/Publisher), 420 N. 5th Street/Suite 910, Minneapolis, MN 55401, in a first edition of 1,200 copies.

To
The Memory of My Aunt
Anna Schroepfer
August, 1910 – February, 1930

CONTENTS

TWO CARS

There. I look up from my desk, out the window and see a funeral procession is just going by on Lexington Parkway in St. Paul. Normal traffic resumes. Except I never consider it to be: normal. Somewhere inside where I still live in the small town; where those things I knew then, still are; that part of me thinks a normal flow of traffic means:

One or two 1949 Fords, both black, passing by, one in mid-morning, one in late afternoon, causing a small girl to look up from studying cracks in the sidewalk.

UNDER THE GRAND PIANO

I grew up under my mother's grand piano. Sitting cross-legged on the floor, I would look up into the maze of niches and cubbyholes. I kept things in them. A red velvet box. It was long and narrow. My father had given my mother a watch in this, but I used it to hold funerals. Under the black piano. When I was five.

There were times I stayed there while someone was at the keyboard. When it was my sister, especially my sister working on Rachmaninoff or Tchaikovsky, then it was like this: Running to stand beneath the underpass at that moment when the steam engine arrived overhead; the whole long train bearing down and passing, right over my head.

THE STEAM ENGINE

When that glorious and terrifying black monster of a steam engine bore down on our town, I would stand as close as I dared, eyes squeezed shut, against the cinders, against the tremendous pull of the noise and the size of that miracle.

Summers being a long mid-afternoon, I would stand barefoot on the ties. Everything smelled burnt. The weeds were black. It was too hot to breathe there, and breathing meant making the only sound around for as far as I could see, up the track, or down. I would wonder how it could happen. When would it happen again?

A person can get into trouble using a word like: miracle. My Uncle Jack did. He and his brother who, as it happens, later became my father, got into the hooch one Sunday afternoon. Just the two of them, alone on the farm, and a whole yard full of chickens. Well, they got to looking at those chickens and before you knew it they had them coming, one by one, up to the porch step drinking hooch right out of the bottle. And their ma coming home into the middle of the whole mess of them, two hours later, still highstepping and crazy:

"What's got into the chickens?"

"Odd, ain't it?" (This is my Uncle Jack talking now.) "It just *came* on 'em, like a miracle." Miracle their ass. Which is where they caught it.

Miracle was the worst possible word to use on that woman. She spent half her life on her knees in the church. Any woman does that knows better than to believe in miracles.

So I don't want you to think I don't know I'm in trouble with a word like: miracle. And how I stood as close to it as I dared.

MY GRANDFATHER'S EYES

Then too, there was some fuss that day about whether or not I could button his shoes. He said no, that I could not, but I persisted, then bent to the task of it. I did say button, not lace or tie, because that's how shoes were then and made of leather, too, with buttons the size of pearls in one black row. I thought of using the quick, deft hook made for taking hold of the button exactly and drawing it through the eyelet, but I did not, wanting instead to give my fingers the feel of those buttons. I might have laid my head on his knee, then. It was only a moment before, (I was three, or four, not yet five), he had held me on his lap, letting me tug his white mustache and look carefully for the blue vein that ran up the side of his temple. His ears were large and his eyes had that quiet, removed blue I had only just discovered in the skies. How came this blue into my grandfather's eyes? I did not know and could only bend down absorbed, intent on buttoning his shoes.

MONDAY

On Monday morning my mother did the laundry at a wringer washer in an unfinished basement. We were a family of five and although she began it early before I was up, I knew even then, when I was four or five, that I could count on the steam and each load and the mounds of clothes to keep her through the whole long morning. My brother and sister would leave for school. My father would slurp his coffee staring straight ahead, then remove his glasses from a desk drawer in the living room, adjust them on his face, and leave for the barbershop. Then, except for the churn and thug of that washer machine motor in the basement, the house fell silent. And it was a falling; a settling down into a precise kind of stillness that I would then enter. I went into it: with the tables; the chairs; with the grand piano, curved and black; with the light that split through leaded glass into bands of color on the complex, flowered pattern of the rug. Even the dust, visible in certain strong shafts of sunlight, was engaged in the active process of settling. This, as far as I know, was my first introduction to the life of the moment.

THE BARBER

My father's barbershop is under a bank. It is a two-chair shop but he has always worked alone. Out back is a garbage can full of hair. He keeps a clean shop. This is why there is always a fine sifting of slivers of hair on the ashtrays, and the table with magazines, and the showcase with shampoos for sale. His tools lie on a counter behind the chair at which he usually works: fine and wide-toothed combs; two clippers; four or five scissors.

Most often I was in his shop after hours, in company with the silence of the tools, remembering how he would put his hand to the scissors.

LATHER

A man, usually an old man, more often than not a tired man, comes into my father's shop. He sits in the barber's chair. The man leans back, but my father is lowering the back as he leans. The chair is falling backward and the man with it, until his head stops, level with his feet stretched out in front of him. Bulk settles. My father turns on the tap. Steam rises from the bowl and he sinks a towel, a white towel, into the water, working it into a twist. He squeezes. More. Until no more water drips from the tight ring, steam caught in every turn of it. He unwraps this, while wrapping it around the face of the man, who is not sleeping. Firmly, with the middle of the towel making a white cup to cradle the man's chin, he pats it up and around the man's face, lying end over end at the fore of the skull. The barber wets a second towel. Is the man dead? The wetting and the squeezing take long, each time, long, and I see the man is breathing. The barber uses only two towels, but the man has had four different steam packs, each one arriving up to temperature at his face. Something will happen next. I feel it on behalf of the man who lies with his hands under the cloth. I can see them folded on his stomach.

THE RAT

This is the morning now, at first coffee, and I am wondering: Where were you before you were five? What city? What mornings? How did it go, your life in the house and out? I am asking, not because these are things we 'remember' in some idle and curious way, but because it remains vital and active in us. Our life at three and four and five continues, even now, and so I want to know: What was it then? What is it now?

My perimeters were limited up to the age of five. No going beyond the range of those houses immediate to our alley, and No Crossing the Street. There was but one other little girl whose life also fell within that range and her name was Kathleen. She was sharp featured and spoke in sprays: I'm NeverNeverNever going to play with you again. But then, there we would be within the half hour, back at one another's porch step, rattling the screen door: Can Kathleen come out to play? I was never sure if she would answer her door.

Those were the days of huge backyard gardens and barns still in use. Some of our neighbors kept chickens. Life was a mix of tillage and scratching and fodder. It went on, above as well as below ground. Once, while I was waiting, somewhat anxiously as always, for Kathleen to answer her door, or not, I saw in the low weeds near the neighbor's basement window a large brown rat, not moving, with its eye fixed on me. That moment still goes on for me. I cannot tell you what happens next. I do know one other thing. At this same moment, sitting to the right just inside the screen door I am pounding on, is Kathleen's grandfather. He sits on a chair in the kitchen, and his mouth hangs open. He has lockjaw, and has come to live with his daughter, Kathleen's mother, so she can care for him while he is dying of it, which will not take long.

HOT AND COLD RUNNING WATER

One morning, the icebox was gone. I already knew the refrigerator; how it stood round-shouldered and white among us in the kitchen. I didn't know the icebox had to go. And with it the man who worked the tongs, hinged and clamped onto blocks of ice leaving a trail of chips we could count on in the summer.

Then, just as suddenly: hot and cold running water. The tin wash tub disappeared along with the steam rising from the tea kettle boiling water to mix with a tubful of cold on a Saturday night. Gone, the shift of variables that went into making the bath, its final temperature the constant: Surprise.

THE PIANO TUNER

The man who tuned the piano would come at the change of season, always without warning. He arrived as if expected, pushing through half-closed doors, coming in among us like an old wound in constant fester giving off an odor of irritation. Dogs and children picked it up, scattering at first scent. Why our mothers were nice to him, we did not know; some said it was because he was nice to pianos. He worried the strings, one by one, stopping at regular intervals to talk with anyone nearby. If he smiled (a terrible thing to see) it was because he wanted you to agree with him.

He is gone now, but his absence resides. As if I carry it in an ailing tooth that I worry with my tongue. Perhaps even in all of my teeth, worrying them, one by one.

THE GOLD RADIATOR

Where I saw the gold radiator was, in fact, in the jewelry shop. It was in the back where the jeweler's brother ran his optometry business. This was separated from the rest of the shop by a curtain hung on wooden rings that rattled when he closed it, coughing, and about to come toward you and your troublesome eyes. I was very young when I began it, going there, and the radiator was along the wall to my right as I sat in the chair that was too far away from everything I was trying to see. He would hold the different lenses in front of my eyes, sometimes breathing on my cheek. It would take a long time, and his breathing would increase with his frustration, flicking the lenses faster and faster in front of my eyes, making the radiator jump in and out of focus, peripherally, wavering gold between me and everything I couldn't see.

SIDEWALKS

Well. Think of the sidewalks, then.

I don't want to think of the sidewalks. It was dull.

Precisely.

As you will. The sidewalks ran north and east and south and west. Go on.

That's what I'm telling you. There was nowhere to go on them *to*.

Not that. Go on with the sidewalks. What about the sidewalks?

Jesus Christ. The sidewalks. The sidewalks were made of concrete and I flew over them like a bloody bird.

Don't be flip. Concrete is a good start.

No, it isn't. Concrete isn't a good start for anything. Especially not sidewalks. It cracks.

I thought you'd get to that, but not quite this soon. Go on.

THE TRUTH

There were two ways to get to my grandmother's house. One was to cross the railroad tracks and go on down the block past the white clapboard building where the tailor had his shop; turn right down the alley which turns again left and rutted up to Mrs. Shebetka's back door where you could stop, standing in view of my grandma's back porch. If you stood there in the summer, her neighbor's garden was mean and small, over-shadowed by a row of hot, horny sunflowers, tall as a grown man and grabbing for their share of the air. The row belonged to my grandmother, widowed and fertile.

The other way was through the underpass along Highway 4, across Main Street and down a block of nothing to the alley; turn left past Bill Keyes's house and hope crazy old Bill won't come out; cut around my grandma's barn and up the skinny back walk where my grandpa died: pushed over by a huge stray dog, the walk being brick, it killed him.

Most often I went the first way, up to the back door. Go ahead. Kick it in. The smells of garlic and camphor will no longer assail you. The kitchen belongs to someone else now, but you wouldn't find the truth there anyway. Stick to the corner of Shebetka's house. Go on. Walk back out to the initial spot and stand, rooted. Do not move. Feel the sharp edge of that house's corner where wall meets wall. That's it. Turn right, now. Turn into the sunflowers. You are tall as a grown woman looking into your grandmother's grey-green eyes. In the yellow heat of the sunflower patch you are aware of her strength, the diffusion of countless spores flying thick in the air like fine dust swelling your nostrils. Breathe deep.

BESLER

Besler was an apothecary from Nürnberg who was in charge of the gardens belonging to Conrad, Prince Bishop of Eichstatt. In addition to his regular duties, Besler took on the task of drawing and recording every variety of plant grown in the garden. The resulting large and magnificently detailed engravings and text are arranged according to the seasonal progression of bloom. The project took sixteen years to complete, resulting in one of the most massive and decorative of all books in botanical literature. The plant shown is the Common Sunflower.

—from the New York Botanical Garden Poster Series, 1975

So Besler.

What made you do it? What comprised a day in Eichstatt in 1613 to allow an arrangement 'according to the seasonal progression of bloom'? What candles burned at night, or how late into the night? Born Basilius Besler, did you keep a hound? Did you have a great dog panting at your side or deep in daily slumber breathing in and out to the scratch of your pen on paper? How did you come by that name, the sound of each syllable pushing softly on the next? There are small bells ringing in your name, Basilius Besler.

Christened.

I am occupied with the hour, Besler, and with the light. How did you regard the day? Something did not hurry you, since we have these 'large and magnificently detailed engravings' that came from your eye through an impulse down the arm and out the fingers working the pen. It must have been pen. Look at the crosshatching on this leaf of the Common Sunflower. I am looking just now into the face of a flower drawn exactly as it grew in the gardens of Conrad that summer of 1613.

Christened, Basilius.

Did you cry, startling at the water poured over your forehead disturbing an early sleep so we could call you by name? And after, with the day gone, during those moist hours of dark, your young mother woke, tired and eager to lift you to her breast. Some tree was growing in that hour, under moonlight or not, its leaves moving.

Besler, Apothecary

How was it you 'took on the task'? Which day did it begin; in what hour? The face of this flower is under direct illumination. Put your foot down at noon and there is no shadow. (I am tracking you, Besler). If it was noon, if the hunger for this task began under the full nourish of the sun on the face of a bloom, then it would have come all at once. Those of us who take our task at noon are not dreaming. Wide awake, eyes open, what a shock to see without illusion each petal radiating out from the center. Perhaps the jolt made you lift your face for a moment, tip your head back, close your eyes; but your eyes were open, open, in that moment of illumination. A firework; a direct burst of logic not removed into philosophy or mathematics, not the endless variations Bach would give us, the hour of his birth yet to come in Eisenach; but here, now, in Eichstatt at noon you stood, Besler, full in the face of a logic alive in this flower.

Flos Solis maior.

The Library of the New York Botanical Garden, Bronx, New York

15

THE LIBRARY

I had long legs; I was light on my feet. The library was a good run to the south and then west. Wearing the look of a grand old house, it stood apart from other places. I would slow coming toward the great empty lawn, the space around the trees; my heart pounding.

I had to negotiate the door. It was heavy. The knob, placed high, was slippery to the sweat on my hand. I reached up and accomplished the turn while throwing my weight inward. The stretch up played against strength for the push; I hardly ever gained entry first try. Winning it, I discounted the effort. I was in. I was on the other side in the first cool press of the dark, pores open, absorbing the presence of print, of books.

LOST

When the sun went suddenly under, with the wind pushing hard, I remembered that Saturday in March when I was nine and tried to get lost. It was with Cornelius's house showing up for the fourth time that I finally gave in, decided on the front door, and asked if they didn't have any cookies for me. I told Cornelius what I'd been trying to do. I didn't know him well, but I knew he was too young to be in a wheel chair, and that my father went to his house to cut his hair. So Cornelius told me that day, because I asked him: What happened? I wasn't sure I should ask, but he had laughed so hard when I told him about trying to get lost, I thought it would be all right. And it was. I couldn't figure out how, though. How could it be all right with Cornelius that Army doctors used a spinal to put him under when he got wounded; that the wound healed, but they were only beginning to learn about spinals and how they worked, and it worked wrong for Cornelius the rest of his life. I kept a sadness after that. In a town that size where the same houses show up every day, the lives in every one of those houses become part of your life, in some unspoken way. It happens every day. And you can't get lost.

LIES

At least when we told each other lies, they were delicious or horrible and we knew we were lying. Now there is propriety. Sanction. The kind people give each other when the war is over and everyone wants a return to normalcy. Oh, the lies we told! Like the ones I can only imagine were also told, with impunity, in the trenches just before dawn, out of weariness and extremity. Or with abandon, the way children lie, out of longing and perversity, with a great desire for truth.

UNCLE

Sometimes that old uncle, the one whose vest and cigar and everlasting bellow rains into any child's Sunday afternoon a gentle fallout of benign blasphemy; sometimes that uncle is sorely missed, once our Sunday afternoons fall as far away as Iowa, or when we are no longer children. How he would squash his cigar into the oriental bowl on the side-by-side and bellow: Whose funeral? What's for dinner? Where's the dog?

OPENING THE DOOR

The bell rope was thick as a man's wrist and knotted once. I would see it just inside the door to the church where we went everyday before school. The rope trailed down through a hole in the ceiling and, whenever I saw it, hung on a hook to the side. The school janitor rang the bell. His name was Frank.

I was six and near to late. Bracing my feet as always, pulling hard on the door with both my hands, I was suddenly afraid if I opened the door, the bells would begin to ring.

It happened: the door opening; Frank at the rope pulled up off the floor by the weight of the bell; the measured swing of his coming back down; the burst of the din out through the hole, onto the walls, up from the floor, into my bones, out of my head; my bones, my head.

DOWN

Down in the land of the sick and tired, pencils are not allowed. You can bring your poor head, one flat white sheet, and all the fever you can carry in your pockets, but No Rulers. Someone else will have to go to school.

The keeper at the gate is a fierce old woman with a broad and pleasant face, who used to live in a kitchen and be your grandmother. She cooked sauerkraut and grew hollyhocks. Now she sits in a rocker, tapping her foot on the downstroke.

Tap.   Tap.   Tap.

Loud is not allowed. You are given one bed and a window. The bed has a quilt (a quilt, a quilt) and the pillow is full of sleep. There is more sleep in a basket on the floor, and you can help yourself to it whenever you like. But mostly, you stare out the window (Tap.   Tap.   Tap.) looking at the tree. Every branch is there. Your hair spreads onto the pillow beneath your head, and while you sleep, it grows. Silent as the tree with its tangle of branches, your hair grows. You sleep. You breathe in and out. You sleep. You sleep.

THE FURNACE

I see the small girl following her father down the basement steps every winter night after he donned overalls and beret. I see her waiting through the endless grunting job of his hauling the clinkers, tub after heavy tin tub, out of the near-dead fire, up the steps, out into the winter-back-alley-night, and down again for another load. She knows the mounting sense of something in her father as he pitches the first, then the second shovelful of gritty black coal into the latent hopper; each shovelful won with the rhythm of muscle suddenly less and less tired; each thrust of the shovel rewarded with the sound of more coal than any shovel could ever hold, shifting and tumbling itself into some new arrangement in that black mystery, the coal bin. Now I see her leaving the basement steps and standing next to her father in that sacred moment when he took the poker and stirred the lump black coal into flame. I see the moment of flame when he told her to turn her face away, and she didn't.

THE WRITING

My father wrote music. Sometimes I saw him do it on Sunday afternoons, and I was to be quiet. It wasn't hard, or very hard, to be quiet; and he would sit in the living room next to the grand piano he did not play, in a rocking chair, with a rickety card table, no, not standing, but propped: two legs bent under and resting on the arms of the (rocking) chair. He placed on this improbable plane a bottle of permanent ink, into which he would suddenly jab his stick pen and scratch scratch scratch. The tension, in my father, in the imposed silence, in the impending crash of this writing table complete with spilt ink, juxtaposed with the scratch scratch scratch, created a sense of ecstasy comparable only to the coming of that steam engine into our town.

MAZURKA

Chopin never saw forty. Today on the last day of my own thirty-nine, I play his Mazurka, Opus 7, No. 1. This piece is his, although anyone's mazurka comes out of the same rhythm. A mazurka, like the waltz, is written in 3/4 time; but where the waltz is slow, steady and lyrical, the mazurka is full of sweeping movements, leaps and kicks, quirky 8th notes; all the while hanging off the edge of: lyrical. Its base is lyrical, but it refuses to be bound there. Won't stay with it, like the waltz, but takes off. This abandon is the heart of the mazurka. A polka is more energetic, but predictable. Like the march, it is written, played, stomped out in 2/4 time. It has a hidden regulation. Not the lick, the dart, the flame of the mazurka.

I used to talk in mazurka. Probably still do, sometimes. But always, then; and my Grandma Anna would catch my face between her two hands as if to slow me down, even though I was standing perfectly still in front of her. She would say: Stop turning so round and round with your words. You are making me dizzy!

BAREFOOT

Later on, although I cannot say just when, there was a moment that went beyond sidewalks. By then I had a bike. It was blue and I could ride it whenever I liked. This time I did not ride but walked at dusk to the lake not far from my house at one edge of the town.I had been watching the water. Now I turned and began to walk uphill on a road toward houses. It was a dirt road. Barefoot, I stopped, feeling the dust I had kicked up settling onto my toes. It was then I knew: the lake was at my back; the trees, some old, were on a rise to my right in a park that gave way to the fields; somewhere to the left my mother and father were moving in the house after dinner; face forward, that leap and run to the south, my grandmother sat in the rocker in the middle of her living room where she came by way of the boat from Germany. Standing there, I knew exactly where I was.

UNDER THE BRIDGE

Those of you who've had dealings with trolls know: they are highly capricious, can be pernicious, and if you've got one sitting under your bridge smoking a pipe, you'd best get on with it. What A Troll Thinks comes to us not without a great expenditure. Of the sort we pay for real information. Which the trolls have. The trick is to find the source and I have learned: Never trust a troll to tell you anything. They will, but they won't. Most of what a troll says is a labyrinthian elaborating, a musing, a mazing, designed to catch you up. Trolls like to spend time (all of it, if they can) with: They will and they won't. Tell you. Paying attention (the price) to this phenomenon, one begins to get a feeling for the nature of what the troll guards: knowledge of the thing in its element.

Through long experience, trolls have observed that human beings fumble dreadfully when it comes to knowledge. They confuse it with information. Worse, they take what information they have and remove it one step further from knowledge by disassembling it into data. Trolls have been watching this process for centuries, while leaning on the source itself: the belfry; the rusting weather vane; the rubble heap; the graveyard; the bridge — these are the source of real information. What the troll is leaning on, is that which is *informed*. The form is in it. It is the source of: in-form-ation. People see a bridge. They think they can just walk over it and in doing so that they have got from one side to the other. To think this is to be misinformed. It is to miss the form of the bridge entirely. It is to discount the gap beneath the bridge, and in the gap sits the troll. Laughing.

SOME OLD WOMAN

Maybe she wasn't that old, but a lot of her parts were gone. As if she'd been careless with them, left them out too many times overnight or at noon when the sun beats down straight.

"These old bones," she'd say, letting herself down into a chair and settling there in a heap.

You'd look at her and wonder, "What bones?"

One part still working was the index finger on her left hand. When she pointed, it was like an arrow shot true and not connected with anything except what it was aimed toward. Burning, direct, that finger could pick out some thing in the middle of any day, and it would be like this: a barn at three o'clock, riding the prairie with a hold full of animals, bucking the waves. That would happen when she pointed. You would see a thing and then, suddenly, begin to remember it. Like the barn, flying in low off your shoulder to the right and landing on the prairie: a ship, an ark old as Noah's and carrying what we need.

THE BOY

At first there is the note. Delivered to me as I sit at the small desk in a room at the top of a tall house in Cottonwood, tucked into a corner of Lyon County, bordering on Yellow Medicine and Renville.

The boy bends down to hand me the note. He is tentative and dearly connected, still, to the last lick of his mother's milk, even as he grows, lean and hard, into manhood.

I saw him last night with three or four others. It is easy to notice movement in a town so small, so under the sky and fixed to the land, as the land goes on, flat out and hellbent toward horizon.

The buildings in such a town, the houses, sheds and storefronts, are stubborn and tenacious against the pace of the land; and the view down any given alley or one paved street is always telescopic: the fixed corridors of the town acting as a tube through which one scans, even without knowing it, the constant, active horizon. So a movement in the town, any movement, is always an interruption of this larger, steady process, and brings the focus in so sharply, the movement itself seems caught in still frame.

It was so when I saw, last night, toward the far end of town, first the birds, four or five frightened up into flight; and fast behind them, these boys on their bikes, flapping and black in silhouette. How tall will they grow going this fast so soon behind birds? Yet, this boy stops. He hands me the note, even as the bend in his elbow is crooked like a grin, about to stretch, about to break into a full-fledged curve.

DIES IRAE

At age twelve and thirteen, fourteen, fifteen, she walked with her mother in the cold and dark winter mornings to the seven o'clock Daily Mass for the dead. Her mother played the organ, and sometimes one or two faithful choir members would show up, sometimes not. Then it would be only she and her mother singing into the vast, dimly lit stretch below: Dona eis requiem.

There were thirty five hundred people in the town. Of that number, fifteen hundred belonged to the parish of this church. And of those, fifteen to twenty huddled, daily, below, remembering their dead.

School began at eight thirty, whether she was twelve or sixteen; locker doors slamming. She knew some of the others had been up early, too; in the barns, milking cows. But none of them had done the Requiem, remembering every day, the "day of wrath and doom impending".

She kept it to herself; watched her hips get rounder, her breasts, fuller.

HORACE'S LATHE

There was an old man. He died. But when he lived, every day there was the lathe, and it was his lathe. Really it wasn't (his lathe) in any other respect except: he put his hand to it, sometimes. And when he did, in those moments he did, then he and the lathe were one in how they functioned, together. So when he died, in the moment he was dying, he had to let go of everything, and he did not think of his lathe, but his hands did: in how they folded themselves, one over another; the palms, one resting on his chest, and one covering that one, resting. In this attitude the hands were resting from something, and it was work. So the hands were remembering what it was they did, and what it was they were resting from. The hands, in the last moment, remembered the lathe.

There are some here who remember the old man, but they will forget him, or die. There is one here who will outlast the some, even as the lathe outlasted the old man who forgot; except his hands didn't, and neither does the lathe forget a hand. It remembers every time a hand is put to it, what a hand is, and what *it* is, and the two are one in how they function, together. The lathe and the hand together remember the old man who died. And it is the only thing that does.

THE LIGHT

Joyce and I walk during early fall when the light begins its first shift toward a clarity that illuminates each thing. We walk at a good pace through late afternoon toward the lake or along the creek, winding our way through neighborhoods by way of alleys. Our conversation concerns itself with what we see as we walk, noticing finally the lights coming on in the houses; the light going down behind the houses.

Today she sent me home with a hand-picked bouquet. I watched as she moved through her garden, some parts waist high. She was wearing a bright magenta sweater over a deep purple shirt. The cat, her cat, Gadu, could not resist and jumped to her shoulder, settling like a smoke grey collar around her neck as she examined and chose each blossom: a subtle and changing equation of color in the birthing dark.

NOVEMBER, LATE MORNING

In Minnesota it is like this: Every tree stands, all of them bare, except the Red Oaks who have kept their leaves and rub them together in a dry hiss. The Superior Lake is not frozen. She moves ships. Everyone expects snow. None comes. The fields are black, and to every side tall grasses and weeds have turned a slow blanched gold. In the cities and towns it is between Thanksgiving and Christmas. At every outskirt the cemeteries remain the same. Those who have died are in their graves. The ones alive are shopping.

MARTHA

Martha is three. She keeps frogs in her aquarium.

Someone asked her, "What were your frogs doing today? Did you look at them?"

She answered, "Yes, they go up and down!"

THE BUTCHER

It's all right with me that I remember just now the man behind the counter in the butcher's shop who was already so drunk by ten o'clock every Saturday morning he would weave and dip as he hacked off whatever meager cut of meat my mother had told me to order. I stood there with my feet in the sawdust, averting my eyes from the blood on his apron, and the three stumps on his left hand which ended just where the knuckles, long gone, should have begun. Under the age of ten I began this and continued once a week, every week, standing there in terror. I did not know then, nor do I now, whether I feared more for myself or for him. It didn't seem to make a difference. It was all one. Mortal danger.

PIG

I travel into southwestern Minnesota to visit my mother and my father. Born in 1903 and 1904, they continue on in the house where I grew up: my mother in a wheel chair since her stroke of last winter; my father caring for her and himself. I must have made this trip into the hundreds of times by now, and should tire of seeing the landscape. I do not. Perhaps I am having an affair with it. With those fields, each farm, and the tired, dying towns. This time an iridescent shell of hard snow rides the back of the land. One sees cow, sometimes horse; but looking to my right on the road between Nicollet and Courtland, I see pig. A small shed in the distance with a pen: full of pig. Not pink, but a deep red.

ANGELS

I have never met up with any. I think about angels and there are many obstructions in the way. Systems, already erected. Group names: Powers, Thrones, Dominions. There are a few, singular, named angels. Gabriel of the Annunciation made known to the Virgin she would give birth. Michael is Defender, mostly at wars, I think, but perhaps also in the Day of Judgement. Raphael does I Don't Know What, but like these others is called Archangel. I like the word: Archangel. It conjures up for me an image, not of any thing, but of energy. Energy beyond bound, without limit. Also, wing is useful. That image. It belongs to air. It moves in air, on air, and air is something we cannot see. The wing belongs to the invisible realm of air, and so that moves us closer to: Angel.

THE DOG AT THE PRINTMAKER'S HOUSE

The cow jumped over the moon. The moon slipped into a drawer. It lay there etched into a piece of copper sheet; hanging round and low over a mountainous landscape. The man who put it there told me: It prints white.

The little dog laughed, but the big one did not. He slept, afternoons, on the floor beneath the round oak table; the whole bulk of his body, down; the rhythm of his breathing visible at the flank; and sometimes beneath that closed lid: the low roll of slow brown eye. Perhaps he was dreaming.

AYE

Our neighbor in his nineties doesn't remember any of us. Mornings, he greets his wife pleasantly: And Who Are You?

Today I meet him coming down the walk between our houses. He smiles, shaking his head, "I can't find it. It's not here. I know it was here before, but now it's gone. Gone. Can you imagine?"

"Yes," I say.

"And then, last night," he continues, "Each of us had to escort a woman. The women came; we offered our arm. We did a grand job. And now. . ." He flings his hand out, drops his arm. "Can you imagine?"

I imagine it must be a little like waking on any given morning when the night has taken one by storm. How, then, things are whirling in a gentle maelstrom; the eye opening into some center of it, still and looking. How we struggle not to close that eye and dream that we are living.

OBITUARY

Clement Hurd died. Alzheimer's disease. It was in this morning's paper. I clip the article to send to my daughter. Her father had pulled the page out and folded it carefully, placing it on my desk so I would be sure to notice. He did this because of all the nights we read Margaret Wise Brown's *Goodnight Moon* aloud to her, showing her, one by one, Clement Hurd's illustrations. Hoping Clement's pictures would make her drowsy. Would make her very brown eyes close. But they never did. We tried it over and over and it never worked. Not once.

NORDEN

Our daughter, Jennifer, comes home from her trip to West Germany. She has spent much of it, having found a home, in Norden, a mile and a half from the North Sea. Norden. Norddeich. Norderney. It is a music that continues. The town. The harbor preceded by the dyke. And the island in the sea. Cows. Boats. It does not stop. The town goes into the land goes into the sea comes into the land comes into the town and the people make a life by it.

In a house in Norden a child is born midwifed by his grandmother. He grows up, leaves the town for schooling, comes back. He will leave the town again, but meantime has his tools. With his father, the carpenter, he builds houses. The tool box he keeps near his bed. It is elaborate. Pulls up into many trays. His good friend the sculptor has also done his schooling and now for the past eighteen months looks for an apprenticeship. While the American is there, he finds it. The celebration that night in the Borka is noisy. The American lights her cigarette from a candle on the table. People look up. Conversation stops. When you take light from the candle a sailor dies at sea.

THE RINGING OF THE BELLS

We stomp our feet
on the frozen floor
of this outdoor lot

dodging cars
as they nose around us
down narrow lanes

their huge metal bodies
rocking and steaming
under the night sky.

Stomp our feet
and I think of hooves
of impatient horses

loosely aligned
held in place
by reins we cannot see.

Three, nearly abreast
the youngest, a mare
tosses her mane.

I bury my nose in it
rear up and come down to one side
nudging the stallion close in flank.

We are not horses
but move in this way
nudging and stomping

the full human feel of it
large with animal instinct
under the night sky.

We are not horses, but human
a man, woman and first-born child
come on Christmas to hear the bells.

This is a story of humans
of rocking and bells
of cars hunkered down in the parking lot

of the Cathedral
in a massive crouch
on the summit.

This is the story of the summit
and the river below
of the bridges over the river

of the High Bridge
blown to bits
one Sunday afternoon

by demolition experts
who knew what they were doing
who were doing what they know how to do

and the telling
of that instant
when the bridge blew

how our eyes
kept holding it together
even as it came apart.

Together we are come
close on midnight
to hear these bells

and stand among the silent cars
with pistons in all engines
arrested on some point of stroke.

Silent cars
in a silent night
and the first-born with us

her slow red hair
a fire
that we cannot hear.

These are bells
we know by name
and how they came

first by ship
then by rail
from the Paccard Foundry

from France, five bells:
the first called Paul, whose Voice
Does Sound Over All The Earth

the bell named Blessed
that Virgin
who carries her weight

the Archangels
Michael, and Gabriel
Raphael, ringing

The small bell, Francis
who came, a Stranger
Among Us

and the last named John
best loved, that rings
in memory of Austin Charles Smith.

These are bells we can see
free-standing, that swing;
saw them being raised into the tower

watched the man who ran the crane
who understood the ball and the hook and the bell
who knew the weight of the bell

knew it
within inches
and read the inches

from the hand of the man
who stood high up
in the aperture of the tower

his hand turning slowly
each turn of the hand
read like a word

by the man
in the crane
raising the bell:

Come. Stay.
Up. Left.
Stay. Come.

We are come
and stand ready
for the ringing.

JULY FOURTH

Fireworks are a little like war. These explosions. I think veterans watching fireworks must sometimes get the jitters. It could slam them back into war, no matter how much they don't want to go. Reflexes happen. One cowers and dives under a benign summer sky.

Will the bells ring? I hope so. We need them. I thought I heard it somewhere, that the bells will ring, but here is how it is: no one can ever say whether or not they will.

It's like the luck of the lock. If you happen to be there when the barge needs through, then you see it: the terrible churning of the water when the tug starts up, black smoke pouring from twin stacks; men running to throw and pull heavy ropes; the delicate timing of the ropes, securing barge to lock as tug maneuvers in behind; then the anchoring of tug to barge with steel cable, men calling as the winch pulls it tight; so the reverse swing of rope happens in tune to the tightening of the cable, so the final loop of rope is lifted, freeing barge to tug for the push, on out, on down the river: is almost like bells, if you happen to be there.

SATURDAY, AUGUST 10

Yesterday, driving through Duluth, the car quit smooth as the cat slips from under your hand when she's had enough petting. I felt the leaving with my foot; watched the gauge that measures miles per hour drop through degrees spanning downward in the opposite direction of my pressure on the pedal. No matter what I intended, the connection was gone. Try this in downtown Duluth at noon in heavy traffic with men who went directly from mother's milk to boilermakers bearing down behind you in their trucks.

I am not now in the stalled car on Second Street at the corner of impending noon. I am having my first cup of coffee in the morning. All events are simultaneous, and I risk another day.

HARD-BOILED EGG

How about the bloody what do you say we pack it in and start heading (they have maps, don't they?) clear to four o'clock and back before the dust settles.

There are small towns all over this state of Minnesota where you pull off onto the side of the road and park on the gravel strip in front of the bar; where everybody orders a beer and every beer comes fast and with a hard-boiled egg you didn't ask for; where you look down the length of that bar and the attitude of every forearm bent at the elbow is: Shuddup and drink yr. dinner.

THE MECHANIC

We're on the highway and the car starts coughing. Pick a town. Any town. If you grew up in one, you know how to find them; you understand how they work. You can hone in on the horizon from miles ahead and find a water tower, fixed and foreign against the sky, riding just above the tree line. You know you'll find the mechanic.

His shop is in some kind of shed and he comes blinking out into daylight. You don't say much. He heard "how she was running when you pulled 'er in." He glares at your car as if it is a difficult and recalcitrant woman he's been living with for years.

The first thing he does after agreeing to "have a look at 'er", is leave. You know this because you found the cafe in the middle of the block on Main Street, and he slides into the booth behind you. He sits with a man who is clean and brusque. Their talk tells you: this is the local doctor. The mechanic and the doctor. Pie and coffee. Small towns work. These two understand defective parts; they keep bodies running. 10:00 a.m. and they're clinking spoons in their cups and complaining. Happily.

THE MUSICIAN

Recently I found a book of photographs by August Sander. I remembered him as one of six photographers of the Weimer Republic whose work was shown at the Minneapolis Institute of Arts. Sander's photographs gave us an immediate presentation of the strata of society. His were portraits of the people by class and trade. In the book I found every one of the photographs I had seen in the show. Then I found one more. A photograph, not quite focused, taken of a man standing down the road but facing us. It is a country road, not paved, and the man is holding in one hand a small squeeze box, an accordian. He lets it hang down, unfolded. The features of the man's face are not distinct. Perhaps he has a mustache. He looks dark and shambling, in company with the road and that dust not settled. In the other hand he holds a leash to which is attached and sitting calmly, a bear. The bear does not face us. His body is toward us as he sits on the road, but his head is turned, off to one side, and his eyes, more distinct than the man's, do not focus on anything. The focus is in the ears, cocked forward as he waits for the sound of that pleated, dangling squeeze box.

MINNESOTA/NEW YORK

It's dark today, warm and raining. The birds are mad with joy. We came home from this trip to a sudden and heavy burst of Minnesota spring: lilac and honeysuckle; that scent mixed with the dark smell of wet earth, green, things working right and early. And all of this is mixed for me now, with the cherry blossoms in bloom on trees near certain museums in New York; with the ground below those trees covered with the most delicate of pink, of petals; with the wild and heavy green of Central Park; with the dark vein of rock that runs through the earth beneath the city; and more — with the slip and easy turn of streets through Soho; the tangle of the Village; the fenced entryways of the upper Eastside, correct with shining black doors and brass fittings; the tombstones in small church-yards at the early end of Wall Street; the bridges; the tunnels; the traffic on the river; the traffic here, the traffic there, the noise of it rising in one grand horn toot snarl of grid-patterned music plays for me now against the thin, true flutter of every Midwestern spring-hopping bird.

MONICA OCHTRUP'S

first collection of poems, *What I cannot Say/I Will Say*, appeared in 1984. Former Poetry Editor for the WARM Journal, she currently teaches a class in creative writing for seniors at the Jewish Community Center of the Greater St. Paul Area. For the past two years she has served on the Advisory Panel of the Minnesota State Arts Board for fellowships in poetry. She and her husband, Bob Ochtrup, scout country roads in a 1974 MGB and continue to find new access to walking trails along the Mississippi and Minnesota rivers. About her writing she says: "As soon as I begin to make a statement about what writing means to me, I find I am already doing it: the writing. How can I split the meaning from the task? It is all one. It is what I do. In *Pieces From the Long Afternoon* much of the writing comes from images I have carried with me since childhood. Perhaps I write to give voice to the child; to honor and articulate that seeing. When I was a child I had brown eyes. I still have them."